First Friends 2

Numbers Book

Naomi Moir

OXFORD
UNIVERSITY PRESS

Level 2 Scope and sequence

Topic	Structure	Vocabulary	Letters and phonics	Numbers	Songs and chants
1 Hello	Revision I'm (name). Commands	Revision Days of the week	**Alphabet revision**	Revision: 1–2 **Number words:** one, two	**Lesson 2:** Days of the week **Lesson 3:** Letter song **Lesson 4:** Letter song
2 Our school	What's this? It's… Who's this? He's… / She's…	classroom friend music room playground sandbox school bus seesaw teacher	**Alphabet revision**	Revision: 3–5 **Number words:** three, four, five	
3 My friends	Are you…? Yes, I am. / No, I'm not.	cold happy hot hungry sad thirsty tired	**digraph 'sh'** sheep shoes fish	Revision: 6–8 **Number words:** six, seven, eight	**Lesson 3:** Letter song **Lesson 4:** If you're happy…
4 I can…	I can…	catch climb draw jump kick run sing throw	**digraph 'th'** throw thumb bath	Revision: 9–10 **Number words:** nine, ten	**Lesson 3:** Letter song **Lesson 4:** I can jump…
5 My home	There is… / There are…	bedroom dining room kitchen living room lamp plant sofa TV	**digraph 'ch'** chocolate beach kitchen	11–12 eleven, twelve	**Lesson 3:** Letter song **Lesson 4:** Bean plant, bean plant, Grow, grow, grow

Topic	Structure	Vocabulary	Letters and phonics	Numbers	Songs and chants
6 My room	Where is it? It's in / on / under…	bed blanket shelf pillow wardrobe in on under	CVC with 'a': cat hat mat	13–14 thirteen, fourteen	**Lesson 3:** Letter song **Lesson 4:** Put your hand on your head
7 On holiday	How many are there? There are…	beach crab sand sandcastle sea shell umbrella black brown purple white	CVC with 'e': jet net wet	15–16 fifteen, sixteen	**Lesson 3:** Letter song **Lesson 4:** Ten umbrellas in the sun
8 Mealtime	She / He's got…	cheese chicken fish juice potato rice salad soup	CVC with 'i': big dig fig	17–18 seventeen, eighteen	**Lesson 3:** Letter song **Lesson 4:** I love food, let's eat, please
9 Circus fun	She / He / It can…	acrobat bicycle clown drum juggler parrot tent	CVC with 'o': hop mop top	19–20 nineteen, twenty	**Lesson 3:** Letter song **Lesson 4:** Let's all go to the circus
10 Jobs	Is she / he…? Yes, she / he is. / No, she / he isn't.	builder doctor farmer fireman policeman secretary shop assistant (taxi) driver	CVC with 'u': bun run sun	Numbers 11–20 – revision	**Lesson 3:** Letter song **Lesson 4:** How are you today? **Lesson 5:** Twenty horses on the farm

1 Hello

1 Trace and count. Write.

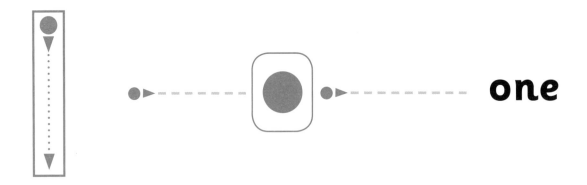

one

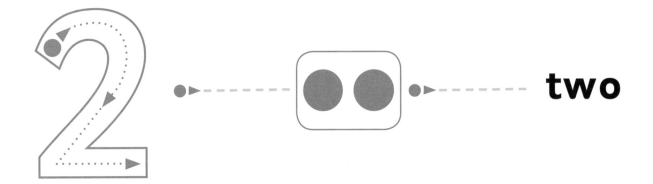

two

two

1 Colour the pictures with 1 flower.

one

2 Colour the pictures with 2 apples.

two

1 Count and match.

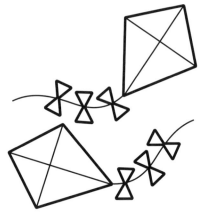

one
two

1 Look and draw.

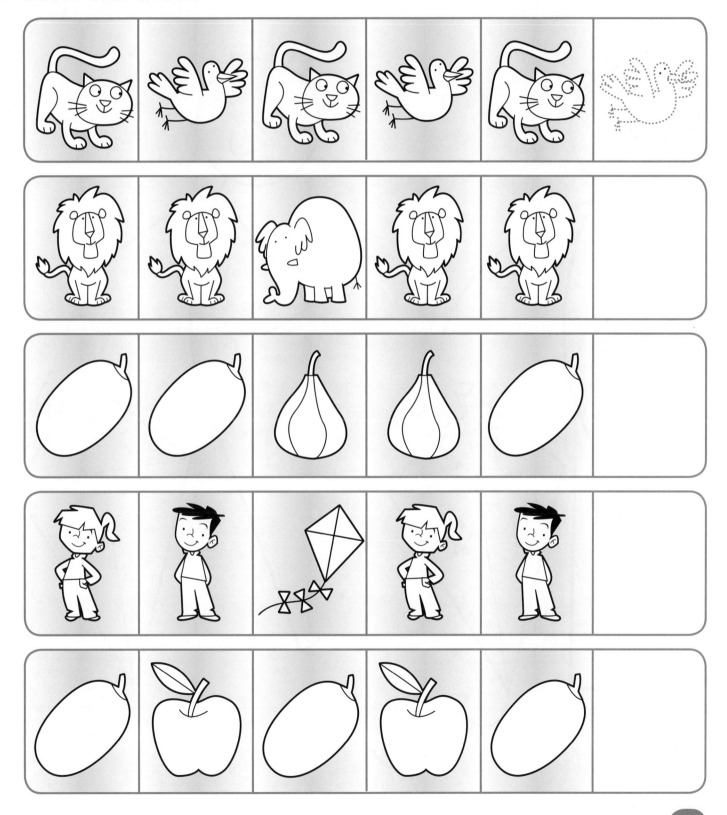

1 Look, draw and colour.

1 Look, count and write. Circle.

  ☐ (one)/two   ☐ one/two   ☐ one/two

  ☐ one/two   ☐ one/two   ☐ one/two

Lesson 1

1 Trace and count. Write.

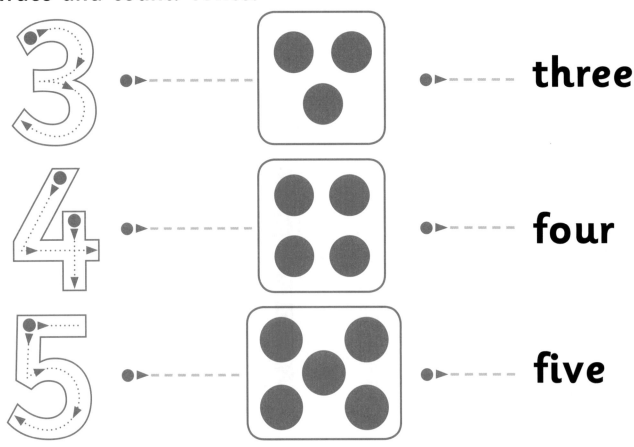

3 · · · · · · · · · · · three

4 · · · · · · · · · · · four

5 · · · · · · · · · · · five

3 4 5 3

three four five

1 Draw and count. Trace and write.

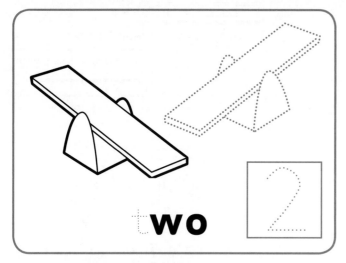

two

2

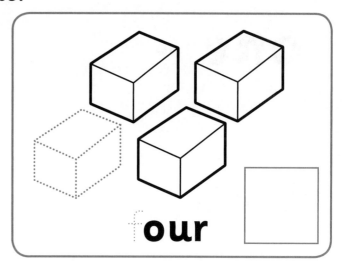

four

three

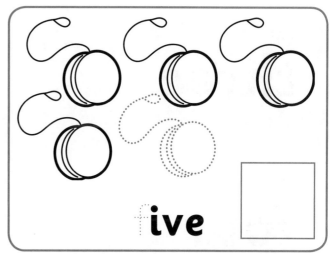

five

three

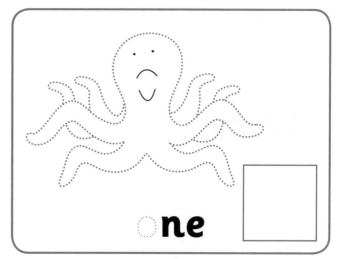

one

1 Count and match.

one •▶

two

three

four

five

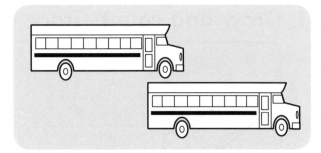

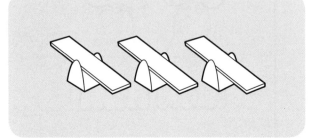

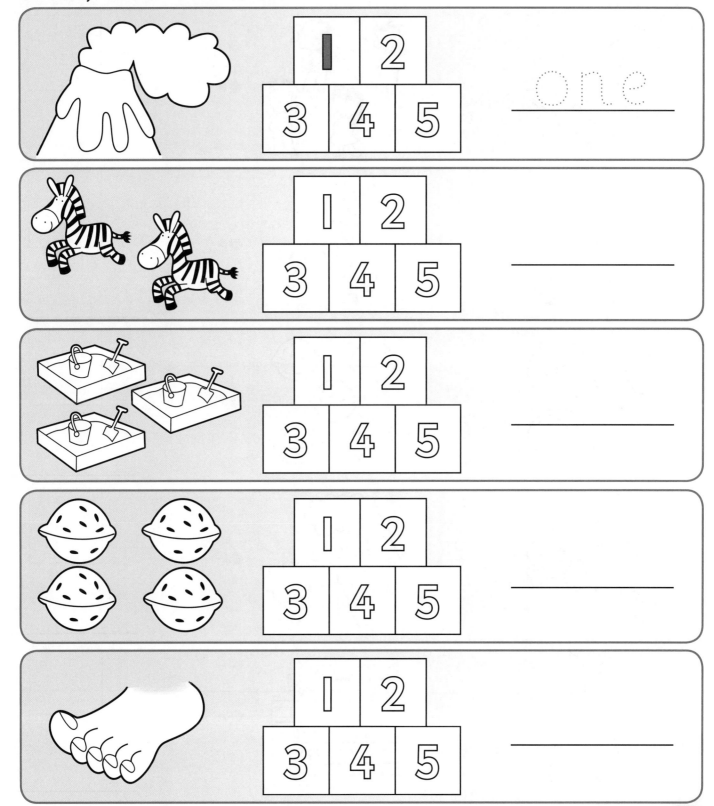

1 Count, colour and write.

one ____

____

____

____

____

1 Count, match and write.

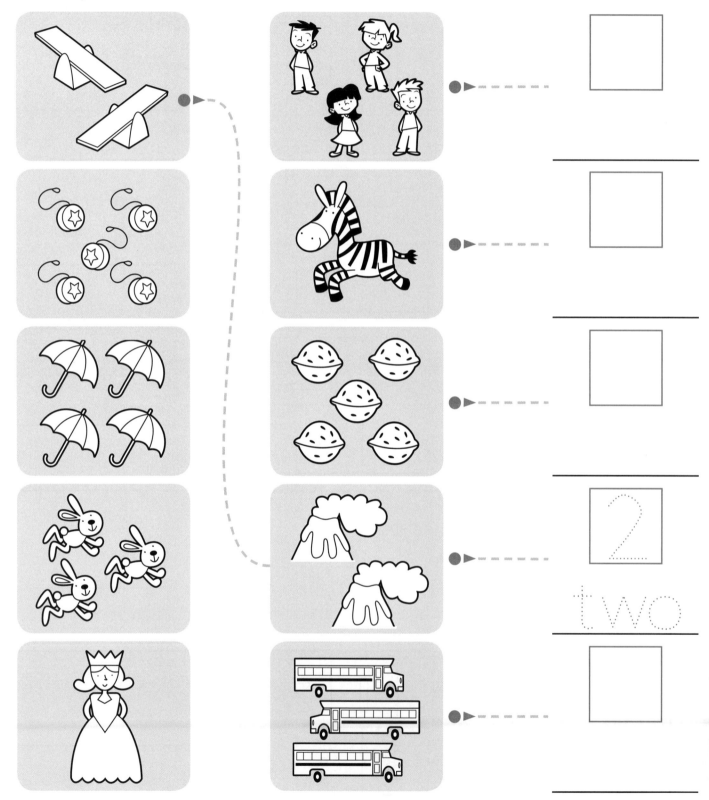

1 Colour. **1** yellow **2** pink

3 green **4** red **5** blue

Lesson 1

1 Trace and count. Write.

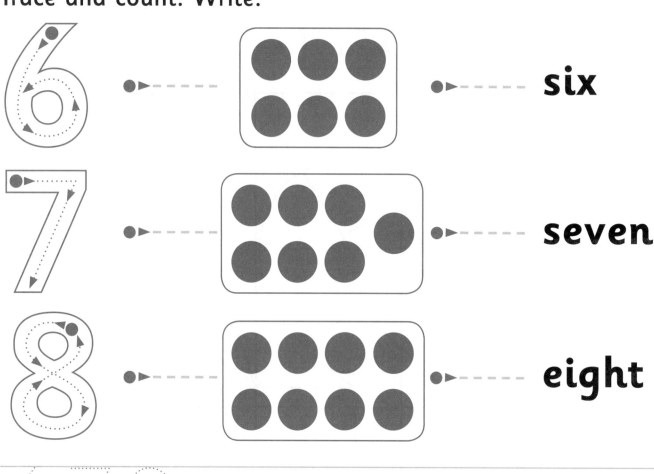

6 7 8

six seven eight

1 Match and draw.

4   5   6   7   8

six   five

eight

four   seven

1 Count, match and trace.

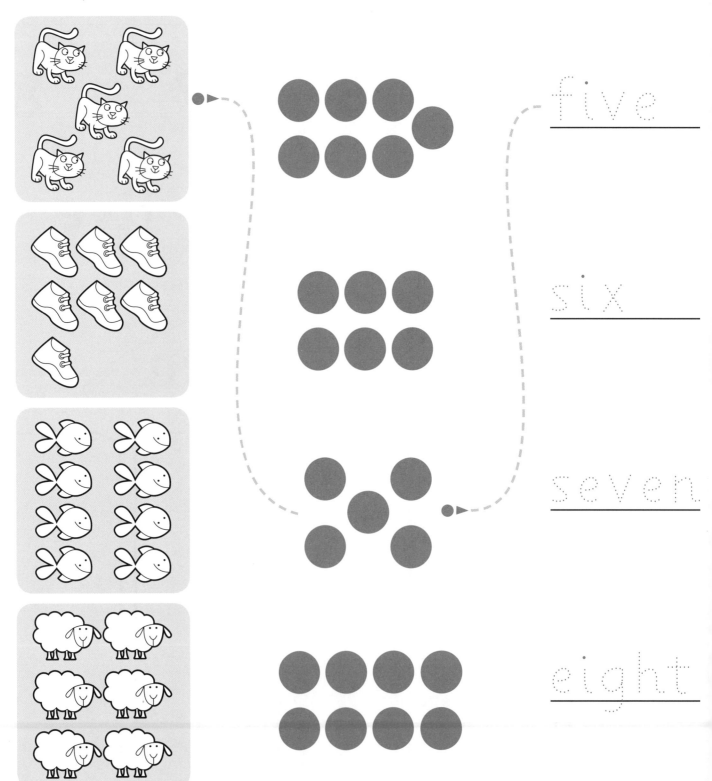

1 Count, write and circle.

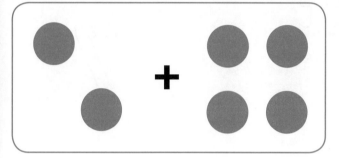

= 6 | five | (six) |

= [ ] | seven | eight |

= [ ] | six | four |

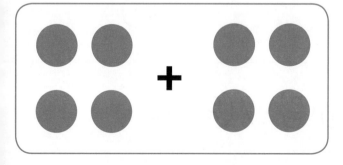

= [ ] | seven | eight |

1 Match the numbers and the words. Colour.

I

eight

7

two

4

5

six

one

three

8

2

four

five

6

3

seven

1 Jump 1 and write.

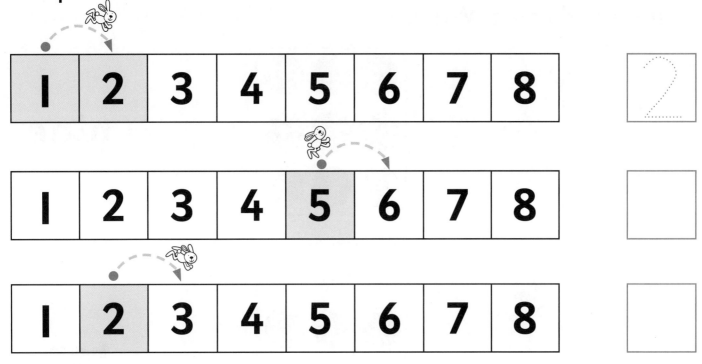

2 Jump 2 and write.

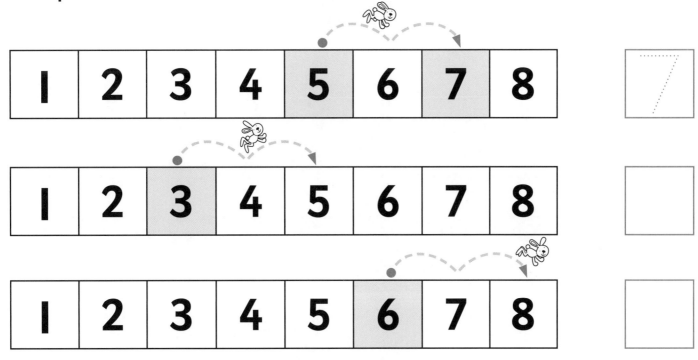

1 Trace and count. Write.

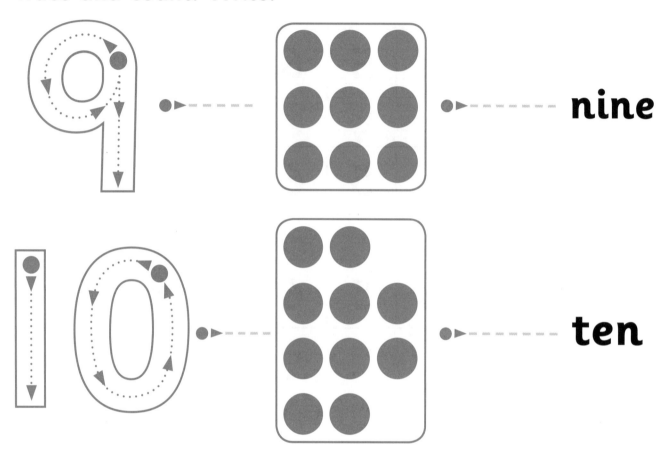

nine

ten

1 Look and write.

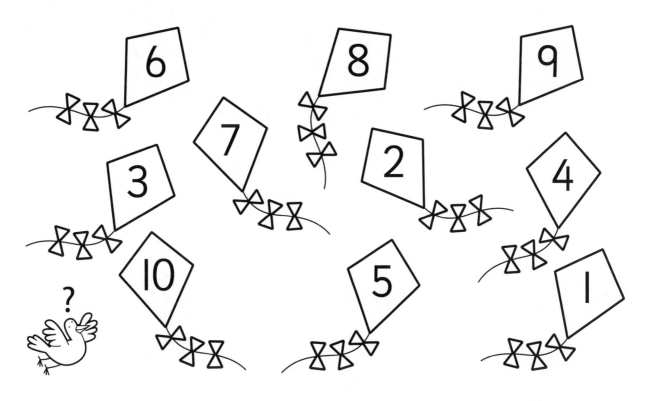

___	___	___	___	___
one	**two**	**three**	**four**	**five**
___	___	___	___	___
six	**seven**	**eight**	**nine**	**ten**

1 Trace, match and write.

six

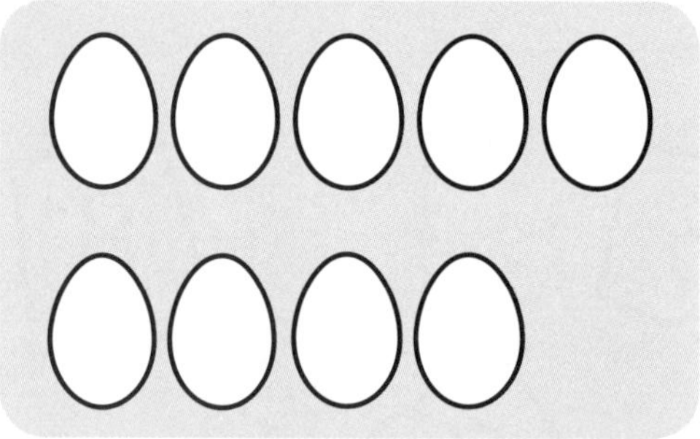

seven

eight

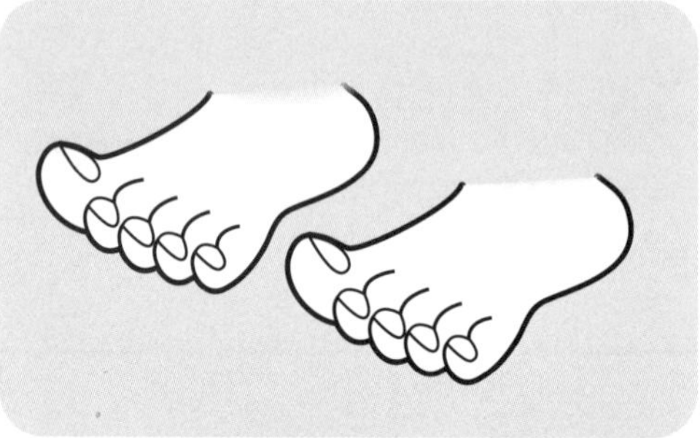

nine

ten

6

1 Look and match.

1 Count and match.

4 + 5 =

8 + 2 =

4 + 6 =

6 + 3 =

5 + 5 =

7 + 2 =

9

10

1 Join the dots. Colour.

six

seven

five

eight

nine

ten

four

three

two

one

5 My home

1 Trace and count. Write.

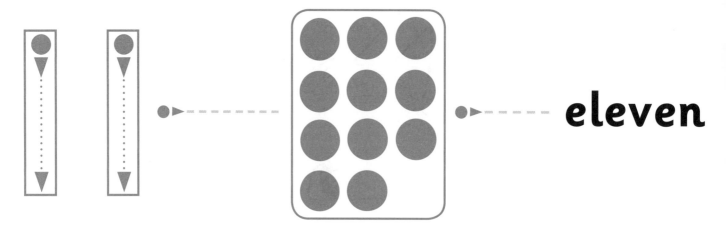

eleven

2 Count and draw 11.

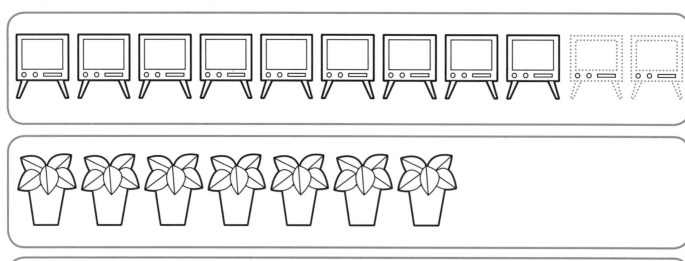

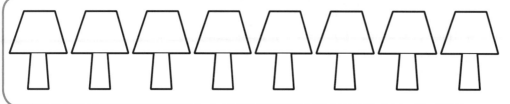

1 Trace and count. Write.

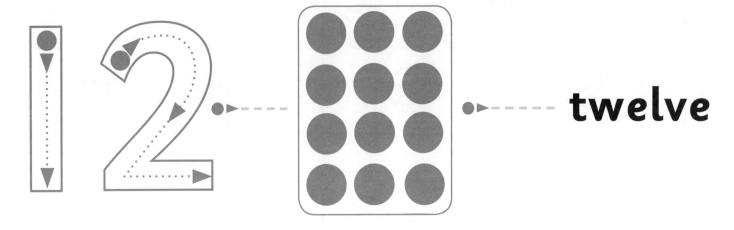

twelve

2 Circle 12 dolls.

1 Count and write.

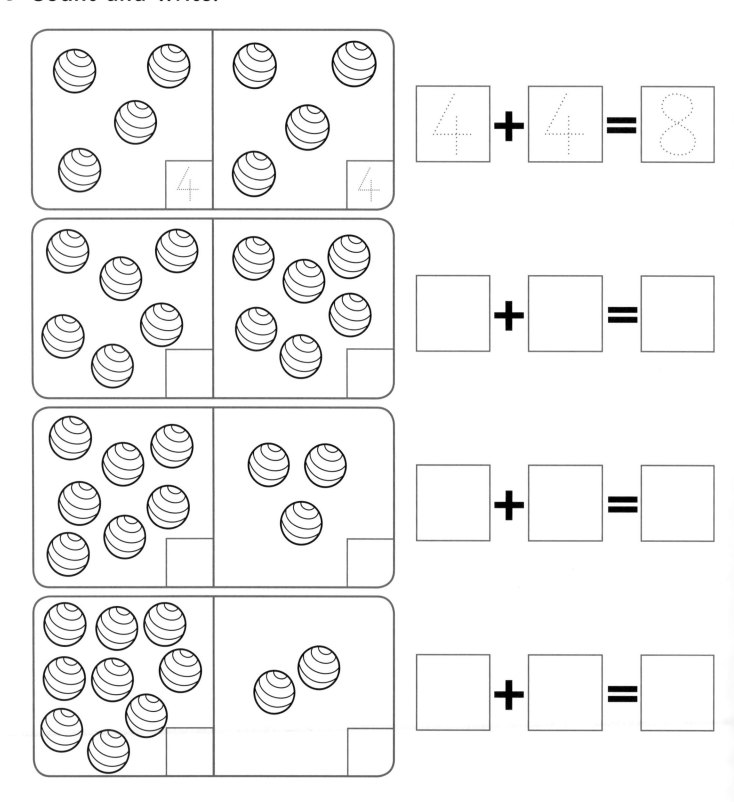

1 Write the missing numbers.

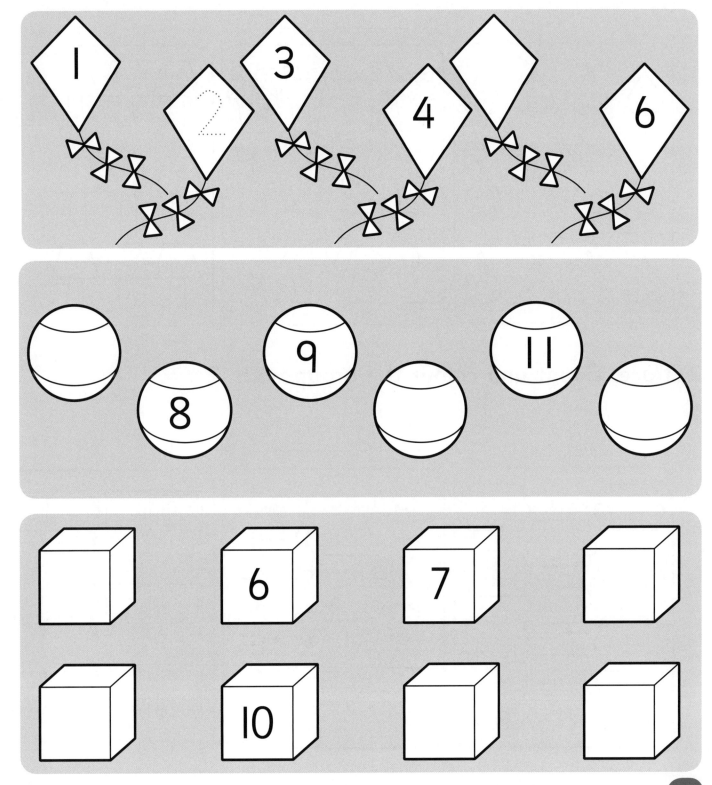

1 Trace. Count and colour the group with 11.

eleven

2 Trace. Count and colour the group with 12.

twelve

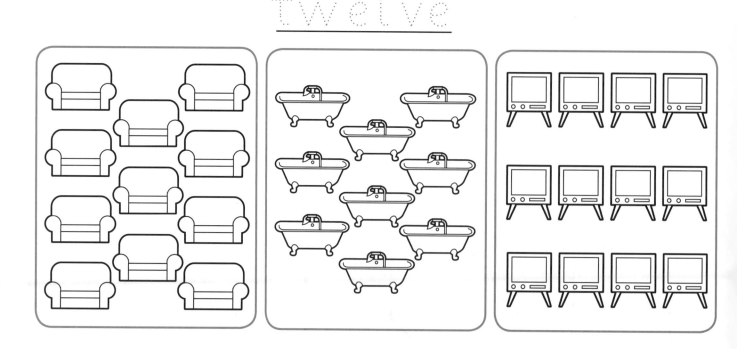

1 Jump back and write.

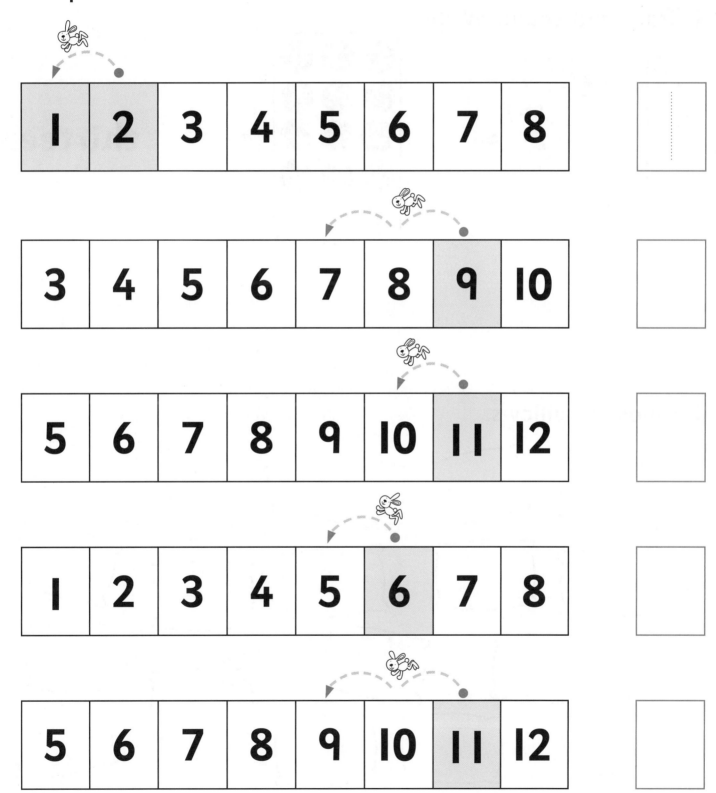

6 My room

1 Trace and count. Write.

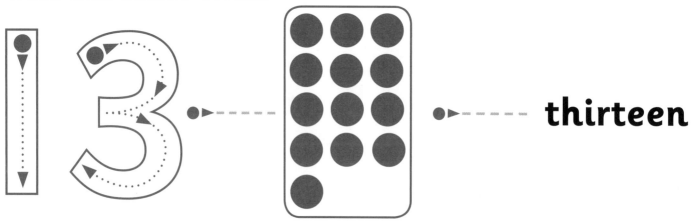

thirteen

2 Colour 13 pillows.

1 Trace and count. Write.

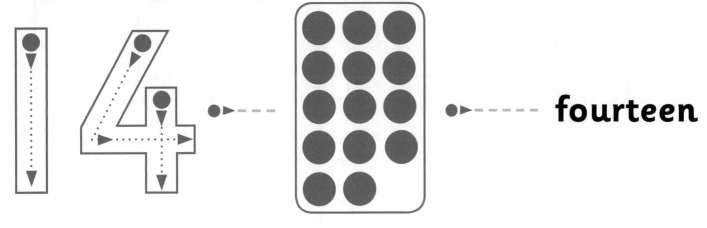

fourteen

2 Colour the number 14 buses.

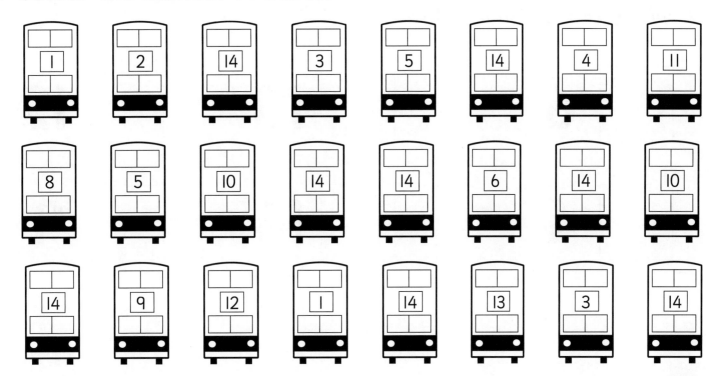

1 Write the missing numbers.

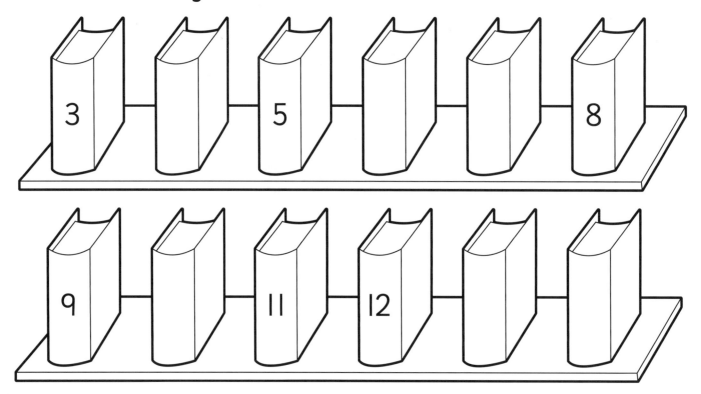

2 Write the number <u>before</u>.

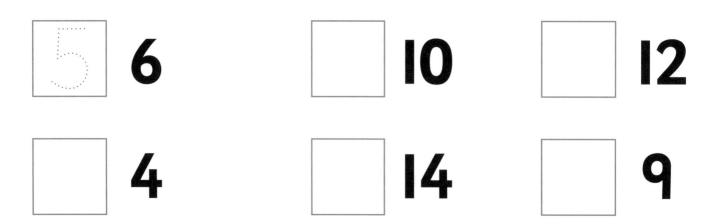

1 Look, count and write.

Take away 1.

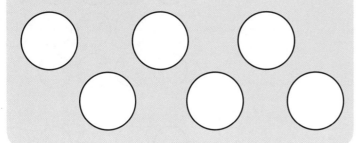

$6 - 1 = $ 5

Take away 2.

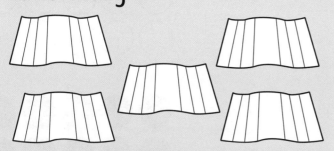

$5 - 2 = $

Take away 2.

$13 - 2 = $

Take away 3.

$10 - 3 = $

1 Match, trace and colour.

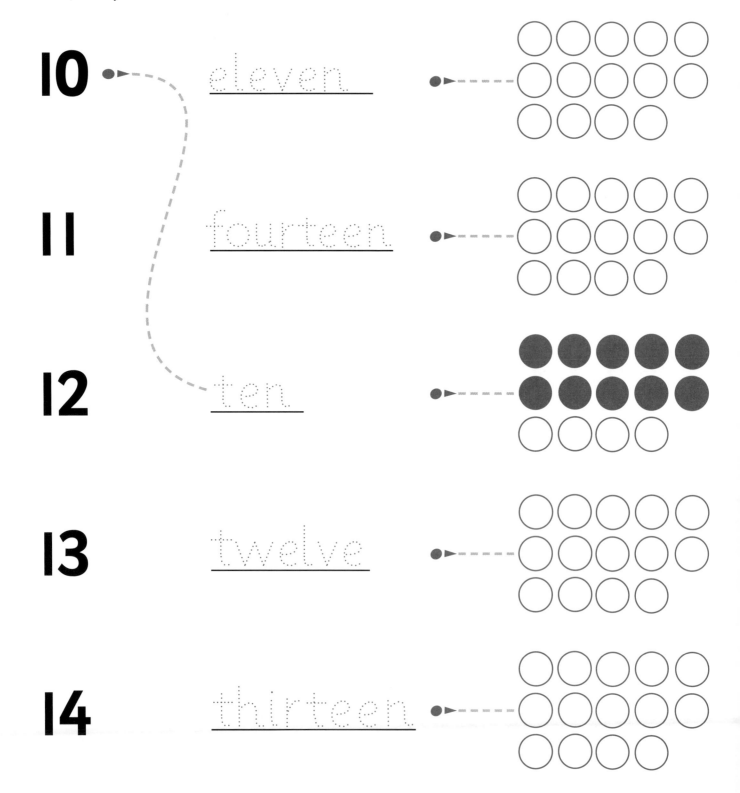

10

11

12

13

14

eleven

fourteen

ten

twelve

thirteen

1 Find and circle the 5 differences.

Lesson 1

1 Trace and count. Write.

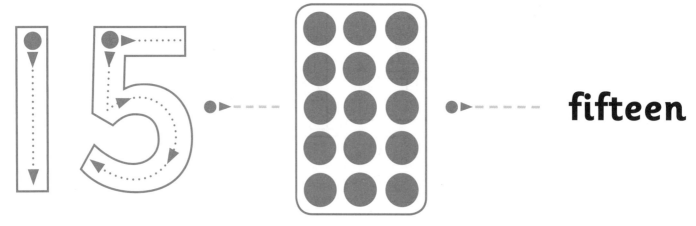

fifteen

fifteen

2 Draw 15 shells on the sandcastle.

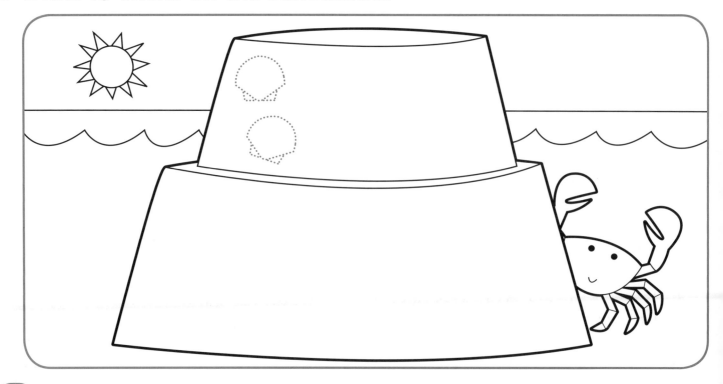

1 Trace and count. Write.

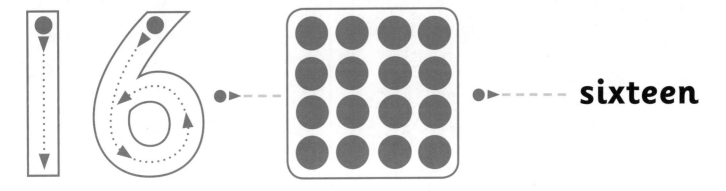

sixteen

2 Circle 16 crabs.

1 Count, write and circle.

thirteen	(fourteen)
fifteen	sixteen

twelve	thirteen
fourteen	fifteen

ten	eleven
twelve	thirteen

thirteen	fourteen
fifteen	sixteen

1 Count and match.

fifteen

$12 + 4 =$

15

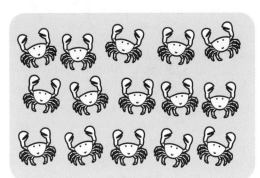

sixteen

$8 + 7 =$

16

$9 + 7 =$

$10 + 5 =$

1 Follow the numbers.

1 Look, count and write.

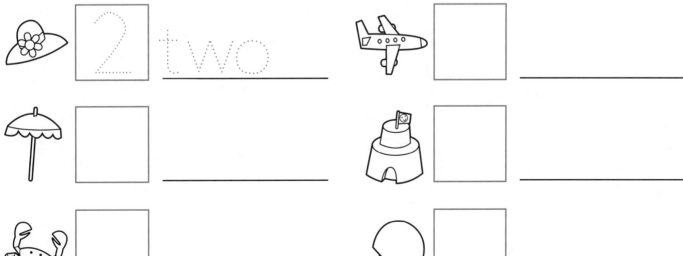

Lesson 1

1 Trace and count. Write.

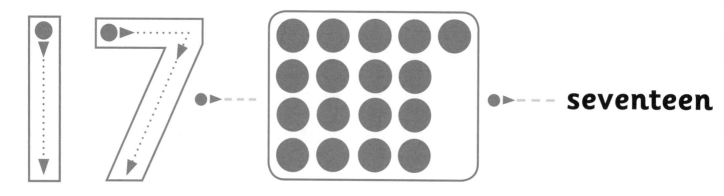

seventeen

seventeen

2 Colour 17 potatoes.

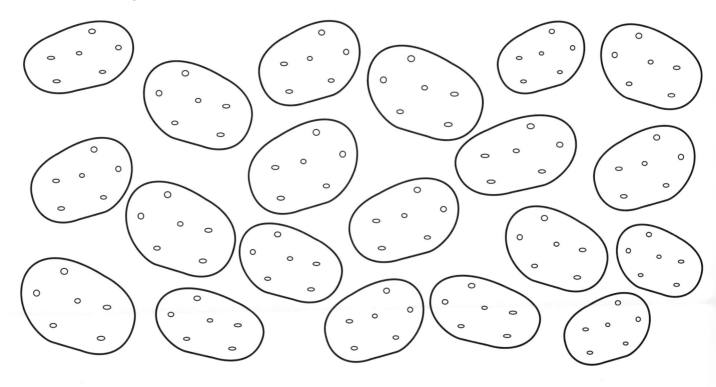

1 Trace and count. Write.

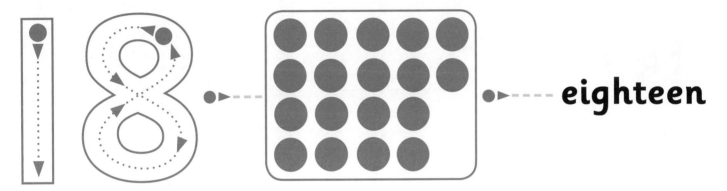

eighteen

2 Count and match.

17

18

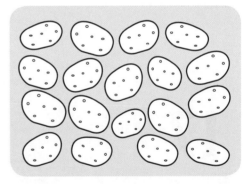

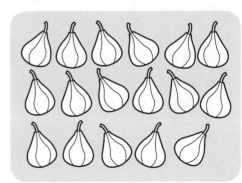

1 Match, trace and colour.

14

15

16

17

18

fifteen

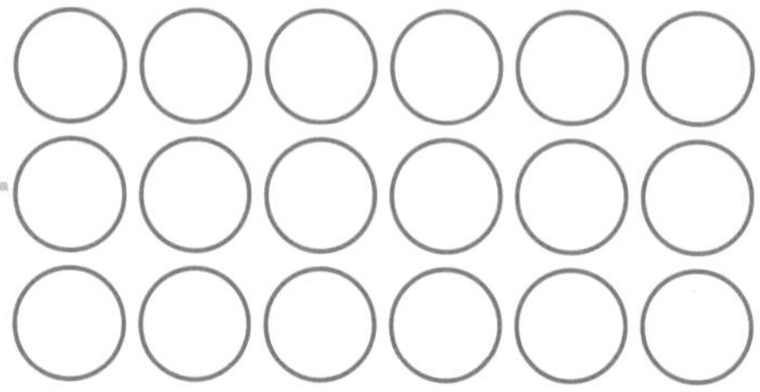

eighteen

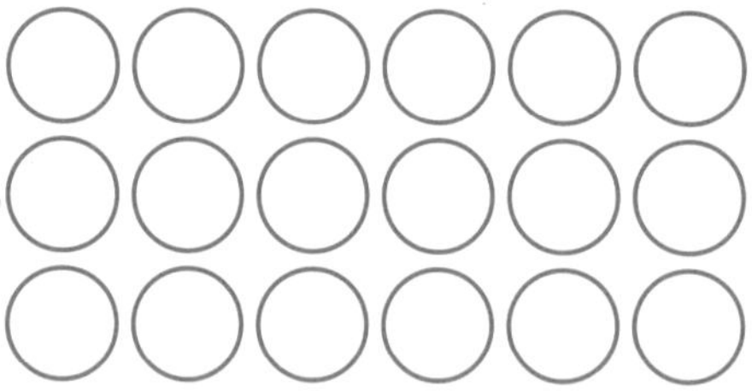

fourteen

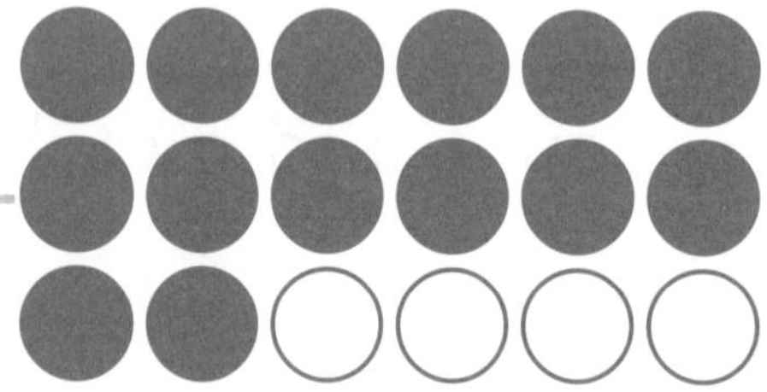

sixteen

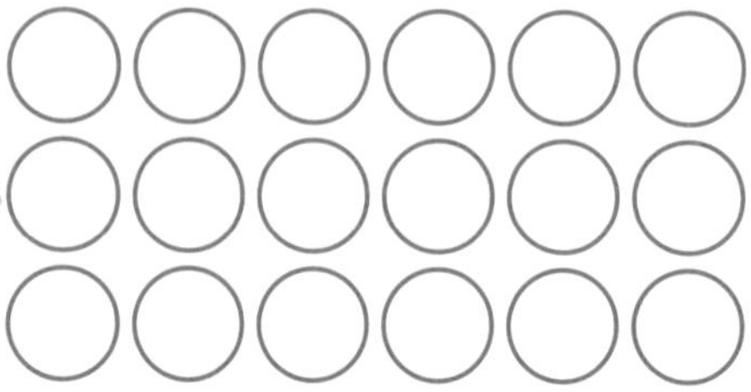

seventeen

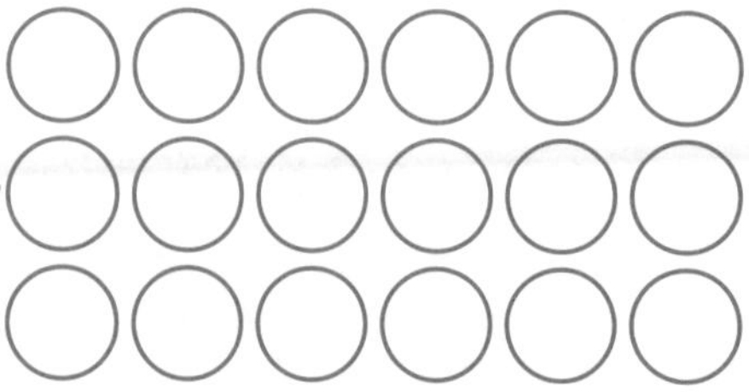

1 Look and match.

1 Count, circle and colour.

fifteen	sixteen	seventeen	eighteen
15	**16**	17	18

fifteen	sixteen	seventeen	eighteen
15	16	17	18

fifteen	sixteen	seventeen	eighteen
15	16	17	18

1 Count and write.

Add +

| 11 | 12 | 13 | 14 | 15 | 16 | 17 | 18 |

11 + 3 = 14

| 11 | 12 | 13 | 14 | 15 | 16 | 17 | 18 |

15 + 2 =

| 11 | 12 | 13 | 14 | 15 | 16 | 17 | 18 |

13 + 5 =

Take away −

| 11 | 12 | 13 | 14 | 15 | 16 | 17 | 18 |

14 − 2 =

| 11 | 12 | 13 | 14 | 15 | 16 | 17 | 18 |

18 − 4 =

9 Circus fun

1 Trace and count. Write.

nineteen

nineteen

2 Colour 19 balls.

1 Trace and count. Write.

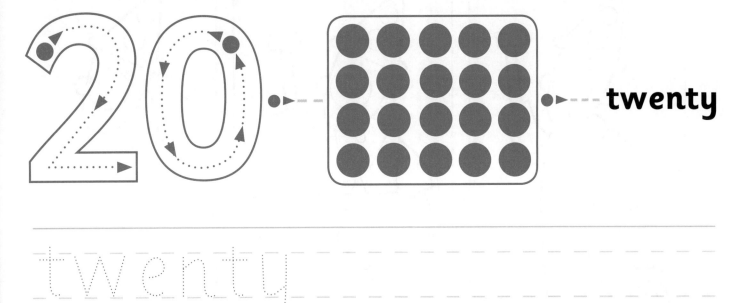

twenty

twenty

2 Count and draw 20.

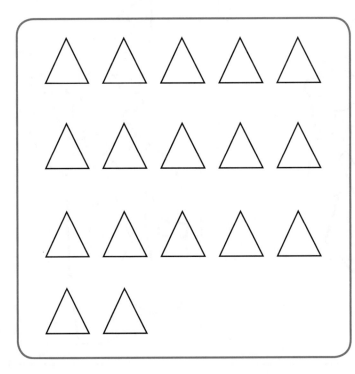

1 Look, order and write.

1 Count and write.

1	2	3	4	5	6	7	8	9	10
11	12	13	14	15	16	17	18	19	20

11 + 7 = $\boxed{18}$ _eighteen_

10 + 10 = $\boxed{}$ _____

12 + 4 = $\boxed{}$ _____

11 + 8 = $\boxed{}$ _____

13 + 4 = $\boxed{}$ _____

1 Write the number **before**.

1	2	3	4	5	6	7	8	9	10
11	12	13	14	15	16	17	18	19	20

15 16   ☐ 10   ☐ 18

☐ 14   ☐ 20   ☐ 17

2 Now write the answers.

16 – 1 = ☐   10 – 1 = ☐

18 – 1 = ☐   14 – 1 = ☐

20 – 1 = ☐   17 – 1 = ☐

1 Trace, count and draw.

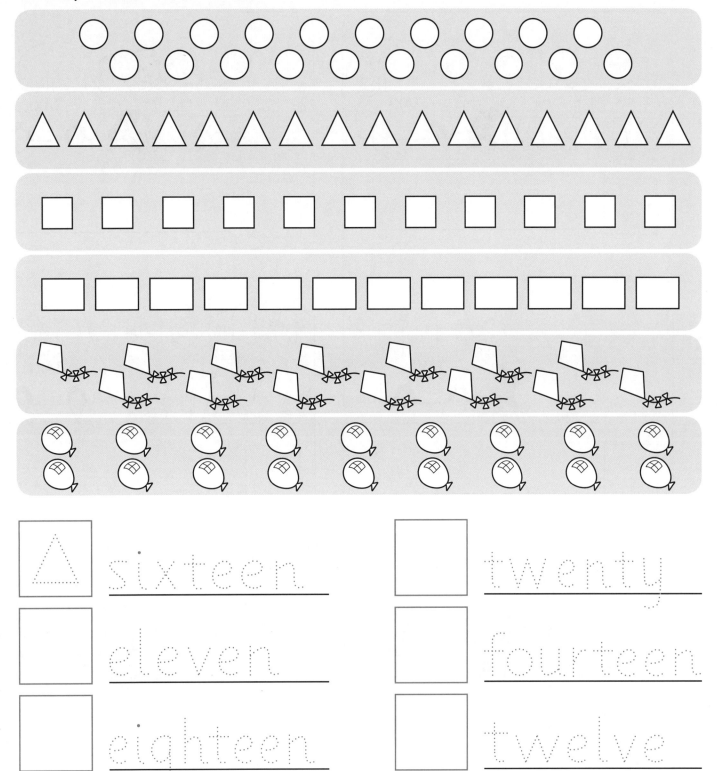

1 Look, order and write.

5 five

1 Count and write.

11 12 13 14 15 16 17 18 19 20

Add $+$

13 + 3 =

16 + 2 =

11 + 4 =

17 + 3 =

Take away $-$

13 − 2 =

18 − 3 =

20 − 6 =

15 − 3 =

1 Write the missing numbers.

2 Look and write.

11	_____
12	_____
_____	**thirteen**
14	_____
_____	**fifteen**

_____	**sixteen**
17	_____
18	_____
_____	**nineteen**
20	_____

1 Follow the numbers and help the farmer find his sheep.

OXFORD
UNIVERSITY PRESS

Great Clarendon Street, Oxford OX2 6DP

Oxford University Press is a department of the University of Oxford.
It furthers the University's objective of excellence in research, scholarship,
and education by publishing worldwide in

Oxford New York

Auckland Cape Town Dar es Salaam Hong Kong Karachi
Kuala Lumpur Madrid Melbourne Mexico City Nairobi
New Delhi Shanghai Taipei Toronto

With offices in

Argentina Austria Brazil Chile Czech Republic France Greece
Guatemala Hungary Italy Japan Poland Portugal Singapore
South Korea Switzerland Thailand Turkey Ukraine Vietnam

OXFORD and OXFORD ENGLISH are registered trade marks of
Oxford University Press in the UK and in certain other countries

ISBN: 978 0 19 443210 8

Printed in China

This book is printed on paper from certified and well-managed sources.

ACKNOWLEDGEMENTS

Illustrations by: John Haslam
Character artwork by: Paul Gibbs.